ASCENDING THE MOUNTAIN

30-Day Devotional Challenge

MADELINE C. HENNERS

ISBN: 1979237514
ISBN-13: 978–1979237512

$\mathcal{I}$ dedicate this book to my loving husband and
prayer partner, David. He has prayerfully and patiently
supported me throughout the creation of this project.
David is a man after God's own heart, and it is an
amazing blessing to be on this spiritual journey with him.

TABLE OF CONTENTS

INTRODUCTION

Then Moses climbed up the mountain,
and the cloud covered it.
And the glory of the Lord
settled down on Mount Sinai.
Exodus 24:15–16

*M*oses experienced the presence of God in a number of different ways, during his decades of walking with the Lord. The passage above shows Moses' pursuit of God, ascending the mountain where the glory of the Lord had descended.

We too are invited to pursue God, ascending the mountain in our own spiritual journey. This 30-day devotional challenge is meant to draw you closer to God, as well as help you hear God's voice more clearly. Some of the exercises in this book may be familiar, while others you may have never experienced.

It is important to commit to this challenge with all of your heart. As I have studied people who have a deep connection with God, past or present, the consistent theme is their commitment of *time* with the Lord. They persevere in their search for Him, do not let discouragement deter them, and keep pressing in for more of God. Give it all you've got!

Also, take time to utilize the journal space. There are journal sections for each exercise, devotion, and throughout the week as you receive words from the Lord: dreams, convictions, visions, Scriptures, songs in your head, etc. When God speaks to us, even when we are unsure it is from Him, it is important to write it down.

When you finish a week or the entire devotion challenge, you will be able to look back and see the ways God spoke to you, themes, and obstacles overcome. For instance, you will be asked to record common distractions you experience early in the challenge, but at the end of the thirty days, you may discover you are much better at focusing on the Lord.

The basic structure of each week contains five devotionals, five exercises and plenty of journal space. You may do the exercises each week in any order; this is to help you fit the exercise to the best timeslot in your schedule. Each week there are four standard exercises, with some variations. The fifth exercises offer a variety of worship experiences over the thirty days. When you complete a challenge, check off the box to keep track.

Exercise one is a time of soaking prayer. Each week there is either an explanation and/or a quote explaining more about that time. Soaking prayer is a time of resting in God's presence, learning how to calm your mind, and listening for God. It is not a time for petitionary prayers; although if something comes to mind, certainly lift it up and let it pass from focus.

Exercise two asks you to immerse yourself in a Bible story or teaching. Find a quiet place and meditate on the passage. Whether you are in the garden with Jesus, dancing with David, or sitting at Jesus' feet like Mary, immerse your senses into that world. Let Jesus speak to you. Challenge yourself to imagine what it would feel like to be there. These biblical stories and teachings are not fairytales, they happened to real people. Often we read Bible stories with such familiarity they loose their awe and wonder. This is a time to rediscover the wonder.

Exercise three asks you to awake in the middle of the night to pray during the 'Night Watch.' I have heard this term used by people who feel God prompting to pray in the early hours of the morning. Although you may dedicate a certain night for that purpose, make sure to listen to the Holy Spirit's prompting. He may awake you on a night you did not expect; do NOT go back to sleep! Change your schedule and respond to the Lord's call.

Exercise four asks you to fast three times from speaking and three times from food. Each time you fast from speaking it is for six hours or more. When you fast from food, be careful to know what level of fasting is appropriate for your body and health. Keep in mind the timing of food fasts; in other words, it is unwise to fast from food on a day you will be very physically active.

Exercise five varies from week to week. Their main focus is on different ways to worship the Lord privately. You may not think a certain exercise is going to impact you at first, but find yourself surprised by it. Have an open mind, heart and spirit when taking on these exercises.

Each week is themed: Starting, Retreating, Surrendering, Listening, Exploring, and Reflecting. The exercises, readings and Scriptures are meant to loosely build on these themes. There is a logical sequence to them, but you do not have to wait until that week to surrender something to the Lord, find your secret place, or listen for how the Lord is speaking. All of the weekly themes should be practiced everyday that we search for God. Do not let any part of this guide restrict the flow of the Holy Spirit's prompting and direction.

Finally, you may be thinking, "Sure, Moses was invited by God to experience more of Him, but how does that relate to me?" At a weekend retreat that I host, we start the sessions with God's open invitation to you. God not only invites you, God longs for you to seek Him with all your heart. To prove this point I'd like to close by sharing a brief personal story.

In the late fall of 2015, I was at an evening worship service where the woman next to me started speaking in tongues. She had prayed in tongues before, but this was different. The pastor quieted down and you could feel the Holy Spirit moving in worship. Suddenly, she switched to speaking in English, saying, "Seek Me while you can find Me. Call upon Me while I am near." As she stood next to me and repeated this over and over again, it was an exact answer to the question on my heart, "God I want to find you, I want to know you more. But how?"

As soon as we were in the car, I asked my husband to see if it was from a certain Scripture. Sure enough, it was Isaiah 55. I made a note of it so I could look at the whole passage later. The next morning, I sat down with my Bible reading plan, which I have no control over, and what was one of my Scripture readings for that day? Isaiah 55!

God confirmed that He had heard the cry of my heart for more of Him, and His response was clear, "Yes, I will be found by you, seek Me while I am near." This is God's response to your heart as well. As you cry out for more, God will meet that desire, even if it takes perseverance on your part.

As you begin this challenge, consider praying this prayer:

"Lord, I want to discover and know You even more than I do already. I trust that You are inviting me on this journey, and I ask for the Holy Spirit's help in committing to this challenge. Take all that I am and all that I have; reveal to me the areas I need to surrender. But most of all, help me to feel Your love, peace and presence as I draw nearer to Your heart. Amen."

STARTING

WEEK ONE

WEEK ONE EXERCISES

These exercises may be done in any order.
Check the box when completed!
An explanation of each exercise can
be found in the following pages.

☐ Soaking Prayer, 30+ minutes

☐ Immersion Prayer, Mary and Martha

☐ Night Watch Prayer, 30+ minutes

☐ Fasting from Speaking, 6+ hours

☐ Humble Posture Prayer, 15+ minutes

EXERCISE 1: Soaking Prayer, 30+ mins

"How do we soak? Finding a place that is set up to be conducive and offers some kind of privacy and silence is the first practical starting point. It could be a particular area in your house, your office or your living room free from distractions. You can have soft music playing in the background. This could help a lot in getting you into the flow and focusing on Him. However, there are some people who would prefer complete silence."[1]
Leif Hetland & Paul Yadao, *Soaking in God's Presence*

At first, the hardest part of any type of contemplative prayer, is quieting the mind.

This is not an emptying but focusing the mind on God and a desire to know Him more deeply. Turn your notifications off on your phone, put it on silent (not even vibrate), and allow God to have your undivided attention. The enemy will seek to distract you but push through those times, writing down things you remember on your to do list, so they do not keep playing over in your head. If you have a spouse and children, see if your spouse can help you carve out this time, keeping the children safe and busy. If needless distractions persist, pray a simple prayer,

"In Jesus name, Lord, help all distractions to cease, so that I may focus my heart, mind and soul upon you."

At the end of your soaking time, write down all the things that distracted you. When you begin next week, start your soaking prayer by asking the Lord to remove those distractions in Jesus' name.

EXERCISE 2: Immersion Prayer, 15+ mins

Mary and Martha, Luke 10:38–42

This prayer time immerses your imagination in the Scripture. Picture yourself in the room, in a role in the story. Who do you identify with? What does it feel like to here Jesus' words, to sit at his feet like Mary, or to be frustrated like Martha? Spend time immersing yourself in the Word.

EXERCISE 3: Night Watch Prayer, 30+ mins

Many prayer warriors have noted the fruitfulness of getting up to pray in the middle of the night. Sometime between the hours of 2 a.m. and 5 a.m., set your alarm to get you out of bed for at least 30 minutes of prayer. It is important you get out of bed, lest you quickly fall back asleep. Prepare the night before to have a space picked out. Pay attention when you are returning to bed, since the Lord may speak as you are drifting back to sleep. Write down anything you receive or feel before going back to sleep, or you may forget them by morning.

"In order to hear God, we must learn to deal with distraction. The key is to be so focused on Him that everything else fades in the background. . . .
      The proper inner attitude is the key that unlocks our ability to hear and see in the Spirit. Watching could be both a gift and an art that must be learned."[2]

James Goll, *Hearing God's Voice Today*

EXERCISE 4: Fasting from Speaking, 6+ hrs

Find a 6+ hour block to remain silent. You may still be doing work around the house, but refrain from playing music, having the television on, or being in public. If your family or spouse is home, perhaps you can do this together. This time of silence is meant to show us the needless ways we speak and how rarely we silence the chatter to truly listen to God.

"A word with power is a word that comes out of silence. . . .
      All this is true only when the silence from which the word comes forth is not emptiness and absence, but fullness and presence, not the human silence of embarrassment, shame, or guilt, but the divine silence in which love rests secure."[3]

Henri Nouwen, *The Way of the Heart*

EXERCISE 5: Humble Posture, 15+ mins

During this prayer time, change the posture in which you pray to present yourself more humbly before the Lord (as you are physically able). This may mean kneeling, laying face first on the ground, or on your back.

DAY 1

1 "Is anyone thirsty? Come and drink—even if you have no money!
   Come, take your choice of wine or milk—it's all free!
2 Why spend your money on food that does not give you strength?
      Why pay for food that does you no good? Listen to me,
      and you will eat what is good. You will enjoy the finest food.
3 "Come to me with your ears wide open. Listen, and you will find life.
      I will make an everlasting covenant with you.
      I will give you all the unfailing love I promised to David.
4 See how I used him to display my power among the peoples.
      I made him a leader among the nations.
5 You also will command nations you do not know, and peoples unknown
      to you will come running to obey, because I, the Lord your God,
         the Holy One of Israel, have made you glorious."
6 Seek the Lord while you can find him. Call on him now while he is near.

Wesley's own experience of prayer
would change over time.
This sermon is ten years after his
Aldersgate awakening.

John Wesley, *"Upon Our Lord's Sermon on the Mount, VI (1748)"*

"Prayer is the lifting up of the heart to God: all words of prayer, without this, are mere hypocrisy. Whenever therefore thou attemptest to pray, see that it be thy one design to commune with God, to lift up thy heart to him, to pour out thy soul before him."[4]

John Wesley, *Christian Perfection*

"Let it be continually offered up to God, through Christ, in flames of holy love . . . 'Let your Soul be filled with so entire a love to him that you may love nothing but for his sake.'"[5]

What would it look like for you
to lift to God not only your words
in prayer but your heart?

SCRIPTURE & READING REFLECTION:

Entry Date: _____

_____

_____

_____

_____

_____

_____

_____

_____

_____

_____

_____

_____

_____

_____

_____

_____

EXERCISE & PRAYER TIME REFLECTION:

_____

_____

_____

_____

_____

_____

_____

_____

_____

_____

_____

_____

_____

_____

DAY 2

10 For everyone who asks, receives. Everyone who seeks, finds. And to everyone who knocks, the door will be opened.

11 "You fathers—if your children ask for a fish, do you give them a snake instead? 12 Or if they ask for an egg, do you give them a scorpion? Of course not! 13 So if you sinful people know how to give good gifts to your children, how much more will your heavenly Father give the Holy Spirit to those who ask him."

This is a difficult Scripture to believe wholeheartedly but God will supply that which He promised and told us to expect. This is our inheritance in Christ!

Michael Lombardo, *Immersed in His Glory*

"Do you hunger for the Lord's presence? Do you long to know His heart? If so, the abundant life Jesus promised is at your fingertips. Far too many believers crave everything but God, and their lifestyles make this unfortunate fact as clear as day. If that's you, repent and ask God to fill you with divine hunger. God never intended for hunger to be difficult to attain; in fact, *it is a gift from God.* Ask Him, and He'll gladly give it to you."[6]

"Don't get discouraged if you don't see instant results or have dynamic encounters right away. Keep at it and don't lose heart. You're working towards a glorious new way of living."[7]

Think of a time you were particularly
discouraged in your prayer life.
That time may be now.
Allow the Holy Spirit to wash that
discouragement away and
replace it with expectancy.

SCRIPTURE & READING REFLECTION:

Entry Date: _____

_____

_____

_____

_____

_____

_____

_____

_____

_____

_____

_____

_____

_____

_____

EXERCISE & PRAYER TIME REFLECTION:

DAY 3

A. W. Tozer, *God's Pursuit of Man*

"When we sing, 'Draw me nearer, nearer, blessed Lord,' we are not thinking of the nearness of place, but of the nearness of relationship.

It is for increasing degrees of awareness that we pray, for a more perfect consciousness of the divine Presence. We need never shout across the spaces to an absent God. He is nearer than our own soul, closer than our most secret thoughts.

Why do some persons 'find' God in a way that others do not? . . . Of course the will of God is the same for all. He has no favorites within His household. All He has ever done for any of His children He will do for all His children. The difference lies not with God but with us.

Pick at random a score of great saints whose lives and testimonies are widely known. . . .

. . . Without attempting anything like a profound analysis I shall say simply that they had spiritual awareness and that they went on to cultivate it until it became the biggest thing in their lives. They differed from the average person in that when they felt the inward longing they *did something about it*. They acquired the lifelong habit of spiritual response. They were not disobedient to the heavenly vision."[8]

How is the Lord asking you to seek Him? What kind of commitment does he desire from you? How might you commit to this process to test his theory?

The Psalm below reminds us of our amazing God who longs to be discovered by us.

Psalm 27

1 The LORD is my light and my salvation—so why should I be afraid? The
   LORD is my fortress, protecting me from danger, so why should I
   tremble?
2 When evil people come to devour me, when my enemies and foes attack
   me, they will stumble and fall.
3 Though a mighty army surrounds me, my heart will not be afraid. Even if
   I am attacked, I will remain confident.
4 The one thing I ask of the LORD—the thing I seek most—is to live in the
   house of the LORD all the days of my life, delighting in the LORD's
   perfections and meditating in his Temple.
5 For he will conceal me there when troubles come; he will hide me in his
   sanctuary. He will place me out of reach on a high rock.
6 Then I will hold my head high above my enemies who surround me. At
   his sanctuary I will offer sacrifices with shouts of joy, singing and
   praising the LORD with music.
7 Hear me as I pray, O LORD. Be merciful and answer me!
8 My heart has heard you say, "Come and talk with me." And my heart
   responds, "LORD, I am coming."
9 Do not turn your back on me. Do not reject your servant in anger. You
   have always been my helper. Don't leave me now; don't abandon
   me, O God of my salvation!
10 Even if my father and mother abandon me, the LORD will hold me
   close.
11 Teach me how to live, O LORD. Lead me along the right path, for my
   enemies are waiting for me.
12 Do not let me fall into their hands. For they accuse me of things I've
   never done; with every breath they threaten me with violence.
13 Yet I am confident I will see the LORD's goodness while I am here in the
   land of the living.
14 Wait patiently for the LORD. Be brave and courageous. Yes, wait
   patiently for the LORD.

SCRIPTURE & READING REFLECTION:

Entry Date: _____

_____

_____

_____

_____

_____

_____

_____

_____

_____

_____

_____

_____

_____

_____

EXERCISE & PRAYER TIME REFLECTION:

_____

_____

_____

_____

_____

_____

_____

_____

_____

_____

_____

_____

_____

_____

_____

_____

DAY 4

Exodus 33:17-23

17 The Lord replied to Moses, "I will indeed do what you have asked, for I look favorably on you, and I know you by name."

18 Moses responded, "Then show me your glorious presence."

19 The Lord replied, "I will make all my goodness pass before you, and I will call out my name, Yahweh, before you. For I will show mercy to anyone I choose, and I will show compassion to anyone I choose. 20 But you may not look directly at my face, for no one may see me and live."

21 The Lord continued, "Look, stand near me on this rock. 22 As my glorious presence passes by, I will hide you in the crevice of the rock and cover you with my hand until I have passed by. 23 Then I will remove my hand and let you see me from behind. But my face will not be seen."

Moses is invited to experience God
in a new and deeper way,
based on his vocalized desire.

How does God desire to reveal Himself
to you in a new and deeper way?

John Stickl, *Follow the Cloud*

"Unfortunately, many of us don't believe everything is possible because we have put God in a box...We try to force him into a box that is way too small...But to put God in a box is to place our own limitations upon him. And whenever we limit God, we instantly get stuck...But God is bigger than your box. He is more loving, forgiving, powerful, merciful, and compassionate than the box you keep him in."[9]

Ask Him to push the boundaries of any box in which you've placed Him.

SCRIPTURE & READING REFLECTION:

Entry Date: _____

_____

_____

_____

_____

_____

_____

_____

_____

_____

_____

_____

_____

_____

_____

_____

_____

_____

_____

_____

EXERCISE & PRAYER TIME REFLECTION:

The writer of Hebrews speaks to Jesus as our ultimate High Priest who opens more doors for us than we could imagine. Included in this is the Most Holy Place.

Hebrews 10:11–12, 19–22

[11] Under the old covenant, the priest stands and ministers before the altar day after day, offering the same sacrifices again and again, which can never take away sins. [12] But our High Priest offered himself to God as a single sacrifice for sins, good for all time. Then he sat down in the place of honor at God's right hand.

[19] And so, dear brothers and sisters, we can boldly enter heaven's Most Holy Place because of the blood of Jesus. [20] By his death, Jesus opened a new and life-giving way through the curtain into the Most Holy Place. [21] And since we have a great High Priest who rules over God's house, [22] let us go right into the presence of God with sincere hearts fully trusting him. For our guilty consciences have been sprinkled with Christ's blood to make us clean, and our bodies have been washed with pure water.

Terry Teykl, *The Presence Based Church*

"In Jesus, the Presence would become accessible to anyone who drew near; it would no longer be dangerous or confined to the shores of the Mediterranean Sea. The veil around the Holy of Holies would be rent forever and replaced with a welcome mat, 'Remain in me' (John 15:1-7). God would reveal himself through the Son in new dimensions of love, compassion and restraint."[10]

A. W. Tozer, *God's Pursuit of Man*

A. W. Tozer claims that every child of God is privileged to experience the Holy Presence of God. He says, "With the veil removed by the rending of Jesus' flesh, with nothing on God's side to prevent us from entering, why do we tarry without? Why do we consent to abide all our days just outside the Holy of Holies and never enter at all to look upon God?"[11]

SCRIPTURE & READING REFLECTION:

Entry Date: _____

_____

_____

_____

_____

_____

_____

_____

_____

_____

_____

_____

_____

_____

_____

EXERCISE & PRAYER TIME REFLECTION:

_____

_____

_____

_____

_____

_____

_____

_____

_____

_____

_____

_____

_____

_____

_____

_____

RETREATING

WEEK TWO

WEEK TWO EXERCISES

These exercises may be done in any order.
Check the box when completed!
An explanation of each exercise can
be found in the following pages.

☐ Soaking Prayer, 30+ minutes

☐ Immersion Prayer, Gethsemane Prayer

☐ Night Watch Prayer, 30+ minutes

☐ Fasting from Food, 24 hours

☐ ABC Worship, 25+ minutes

EXERCISE 1: Soaking Prayer, 30+ mins

Start your soaking prayer by asking the Lord to remove the distractions from last week in Jesus' name. You may decide to play soft music or focus your mind with a verse of Scripture. It is okay to simply rest in God's presence, this is not a time of filling the 30+ minutes with prayer requests.

"Stillness and rest position our hearts to receive. It is hard to receive from Him when we are striving. Many times when He speaks to us, He speaks in whispers, in still, small voice. This necessitates undivided attention and a restful spirit. . . .
. . . When we are at rest, God can do the rest. When we cease striving, He is able to reveal and impart more to us."[1]

Leif Hetland & Paul Yadao, *Soaking in God's Presence*

EXERCISE 2: Immersion Prayer 15+ mins

Gethsemane Prayer, Matthew 26:36–46

This prayer time immerses your imagination in the Scripture. Picture yourself in the garden; what does it smell and feel like? Picture yourself with Jesus, watching how he prays and surrenders to the Father. Then picture yourself as a disciple, fatigued from a long day, full of a Passover meal. What is it like to hear Jesus ask you to stay awake and pray? How do you struggle as the disciples did in your own prayer time? What mercy does Jesus show?

EXERCISE 3: Night Watch Prayer, 30+ mins

Sometime between the hours of 2 a.m. and 5 a.m., set your alarm to get you out of bed for at least 30 minutes of prayer. It is important you get out of bed, lest you quickly fall back asleep. Prepare the night before to have a space picked out. Pay attention when you are returning to bed, since the Lord may speak as you are drifting back to sleep. Write down anything you receive or feel before going back to sleep, or you may forget them by morning.

"Keep on listening, just as the Lord listens to us. Keep on watching, even as the Lord keeps His eyes upon us. Be patient. Keep on waiting, just as Papa God is waiting for you. You will find Him when you do, and you will obtain favor from the Lord!"[2]

James Goll, *Hearing God's Voice Today*

EXERCISE 4: Fasting from Food, 24 hrs

You may do this a number of ways, depending on your health and physical ability. You may decide to fast from solid food, and still drink limited amounts of juice and water. You may fast from all food except a meal at dinner. If you have certain health issues, please consult a doctor before fasting from food. The timeline is also flexible. You may decide to fast from sun down to sun down (i.e. 6 p.m. to 6 p.m.).

The goal of this fast is to go without something in order to refocus our attention on the Lord. When we feel a hunger pain, it reminds us of Jesus and all he sacrificed for us. As Goll mentions below, fasting for him is a time of cleansing his heart.

Ask God to make you more sensitive to His voice, promptings and presence.

"In my own relationship with the Holy Spirit, I often sanctify three days of fasting just for the purpose of cleansing my heart. I am not asking God for stuff; I am asking God to tenderize my heart. Knowing that I still sin and realizing that sin makes me lose my edge and that it loosens my connection with the Lord, I need to take a maintenance break."[3]

James Goll, *Hearing God's Voice Today*

EXERCISE 5: ABC Worship, 25+ mins

For every letter of the alphabet, write a name or attribute that describes God. This is not meant to be done quickly but meaningfully. There may be many ways of describing God using the letter 'B,' for instance. Ponder and choose the one that relates most to your heart and experience of God. This exercise is called 'worship' because you are proclaiming God's goodness. Pray these words back to Him.

This week is about the importance of finding
a secret place to retreat with the Lord
to focus your mind on Him.

Michal Ann Goll, *A Call to the Secret Place*

"We need to find a place to be entirely alone. Susanna Wesley literally had no place to go inside her own home to get away from her many children in order to be alone with the Lord. So when she pulled her apron up over hear head, her children knew it was time to leave her alone. Most of us have better living circumstances than Susanna Wesley. . . .

. . . We must also learn what it takes to quiet our own spirit. . . . We must begin to be quiet by disconnecting from the newspaper, the TV, the radio, and gab sessions with friends. We can then take time to search our hearts, with the help of the Holy Spirit, to find out what's really going on inside of us. . . . But if we want to find the secret place with God, we must enter with our true selves. Keeping up false fronts and masks will hinder us from experiencing God's presence."[4]

36 Anna, a prophet, was also there in the Temple. She was the daughter of Phanuel from the tribe of Asher, and she was very old. Her husband died when they had been married only seven years. 37 Then she lived as a widow to the age of eighty-four. She never left the Temple but stayed there day and night, worshiping God with fasting and prayer. 38 She came along just as Simeon was talking with Mary and Joseph, and she began praising God. She talked about the child to everyone who had been waiting expectantly for God to rescue Jerusalem.

Although this Scripture shows Anna in the Temple day and night, the point of contemplating it here, is to examine her deep rooted motivation to commit her life to this kind of pursuit.

What can we learn from Anna's life with regards to seeking the Lord with all that we are? What must it have felt like to encounter Jesus after all that time?

SCRIPTURE & READING REFLECTION:

Entry Date: _____

_____

_____

_____

_____

_____

_____

_____

_____

_____

_____

_____

_____

_____

_____

_____

EXERCISE & PRAYER TIME REFLECTION:

DAY 7

Psalm 139:1–18, 23–24

[1] O Lord, you have examined my heart and know everything about me.

[2] You know when I sit down or stand up. You know my thoughts even when I'm far away.

[3] You see me when I travel and when I rest at home. You know everything I do.

[4] You know what I am going to say even before I say it, Lord.

[5] You go before me and follow me. You place your hand of blessing on my head.

[6] Such knowledge is too wonderful for me, too great for me to understand!

[7] I can never escape from your Spirit! I can never get away from your presence!

[8] If I go up to heaven, you are there; if I go down to the grave, you are there.

[9] If I ride the wings of the morning, if I dwell by the farthest oceans, [10] even there your hand will guide me, and your strength will support me.

[11] I could ask the darkness to hide me and the light around me to become night—[12] but even in darkness I cannot hide from you. To you the night shines as bright as day. Darkness and light are the same to you.

[13] You made all the delicate, inner parts of my body and knit me together in my mother's womb.

[14] Thank you for making me so wonderfully complex! Your workmanship is marvelous—how well I know it.

[15] You watched me as I was being formed in utter seclusion, as I was woven together in the dark of the womb.

[16] You saw me before I was born. Every day of my life was recorded in your book. Every moment was laid out before a single day had passed.

[17] How precious are your thoughts about me, O God. They cannot be numbered!

[18] I can't even count them; they outnumber the grains of sand! And when I wake up, you are still with me!

[23] Search me, O God, and know my heart; test me and know my anxious thoughts.

[24] Point out anything in me that offends you, and lead me along the path of everlasting life.

Terry Teykl, *The Presence Based Church*

"So what exactly is the Presence of God? Can it even be defined? Talking about presence is difficult because it is not a tangible thing we can see and put our hands on. By nature, it is a somewhat mysterious concept. To try and describe God's Presence is like taking a picture of the Grand Canyon with a Polaroid at night. What you get is a vague representation at best of the original wonder. God's Presence defies the limits of our vocabulary and dwarfs our most unbridled imaginations. Known and yet unknown, it will remain a profoundly wonderful mystery until we see him full of glory in heaven."[5]

What can we experience of God
on this side of eternity?

What testimonies of the early Church,
historical figures, or people you know
come to mind?

SCRIPTURE & READING REFLECTION:

Entry Date: _____

_____

_____

_____

_____

_____

_____

_____

_____

_____

_____

_____

_____

_____

_____

_____

EXERCISE & PRAYER TIME REFLECTION:

DAY 8

Michael Lombardo, *Immersed in His Glory*

"Our primary purpose in life is intimacy with God. Our secondary purpose is the calling placed on our lives to make an impact in this world by the power of the Holy Spirit. Both are vitally important. Both must work together side by side."[6]

"Jesus came first and foremost to restore our union with God. It's your connection with the Spirit of God—through the love and romance of the gospel—that fuels you to accomplish mighty exploits in His name. Intimacy isn't a means to a greater end—it's the crux of the gospel. Nothing else works without intimacy."[7]

Lombardo's point reinforces the call of Scripture
to love God with all of ourselves.
For us to remain focused on the Lord,
our hearts must desire more of Him.

19 "Don't store up treasures here on earth, where moths eat them and rust destroys them, and where thieves break in and steal. 20 Store your treasures in heaven, where moths and rust cannot destroy, and thieves do not break in and steal. 21 Wherever your treasure is, there the desires of your heart will also be.

22 "Your eye is like a lamp that provides light for your body. When your eye is healthy, your whole body is filled with light. 23 But when your eye is unhealthy, your whole body is filled with darkness. And if the light you think you have is actually darkness, how deep that darkness is!
24 "No one can serve two masters. For you will hate one and love the other; you will be devoted to one and despise the other. You cannot serve God and be enslaved to money.

25 "That is why I tell you not to worry about everyday life—whether you have enough food and drink, or enough clothes to wear. Isn't life more than food, and your body more than clothing? 26 Look at the birds. They don't plant or harvest or store food in barns, for your heavenly Father feeds them. And aren't you far more valuable to him than they are? 27 Can all your worries add a single moment to your life?"

What other master or worry is God asking
you to lay down so that your heart may
become more focused on Him?

SCRIPTURE & READING REFLECTION:

Entry Date: _____

_____

_____

_____

_____

_____

_____

_____

_____

_____

_____

_____

_____

_____

_____

_____

EXERCISE & PRAYER TIME REFLECTION:

Richard Foster, *Prayer*

"Jean Vanier, the founder of the L'Arche communities for mentally handicapped people, often explains with a simple illustration his approach to those who live at L'Arche. He will cup his hands lightly and say, 'Suppose I have a wounded bird in my hands. What would happen if I closed my hands completely?' The response is immediate. 'Why, the bird will be crushed and die.' 'Well then, what would happen if I opened my hands completely?' 'Oh, no, then the bird will try to fly away, and it will fall and die.' Vanier smiles and says, 'The right place is like my cupped hand, neither totally opened nor totally closed. It is the space where growth can take place.'

For us too, the hands of God are cupped lightly. We have enough freedom so that we can stretch and grow, but also we have enough protection so that we will not be injured—and so we can be healed. This is the Prayer of Rest."[8]

Read Psalm 91 picturing God's
tender care of you.

Psalm 91

1 Those who live in the shelter of the Most High will find rest in the shadow
of the Almighty.

2 This I declare about the Lord: He alone is my refuge, my place of safety;
he is my God, and I trust him.

3 For he will rescue you from every trap and protect you from deadly
disease.

4 He will cover you with his feathers. He will shelter you with his wings. His
faithful promises are your armor and protection.

5 Do not be afraid of the terrors of the night, nor the arrow that flies in the
day.

6 Do not dread the disease that stalks in darkness, nor the disaster that
strikes at midday.

7 Though a thousand fall at your side, though ten thousand are dying
around you, these evils will not touch you.

8 Just open your eyes, and see how the wicked are punished.

9 If you make the Lord your refuge, if you make the Most High your shelter,
10 no evil will conquer you; no plague will come near your home.

11 For he will order his angels to protect you wherever you go.

12 They will hold you up with their hands so you won't even hurt your foot
on a stone.

13 You will trample upon lions and cobras; you will crush fierce lions and
serpents under your feet!

14 The Lord says, "I will rescue those who love me. I will protect those who
trust in my name.

15 When they call on me, I will answer; I will be with them in trouble. I will
rescue and honor them.

16 I will reward them with a long life and give them my salvation."

SCRIPTURE & READING REFLECTION:

Entry Date: _____

_____

_____

_____

_____

_____

_____

_____

_____

_____

_____

_____

_____

_____

_____

_____

_____

EXERCISE & PRAYER TIME REFLECTION:

Exodus 19:16–20

16 On the morning of the third day, thunder roared and lightning flashed, and a dense cloud came down on the mountain. There was a long, loud blast from a ram's horn, and all the people trembled. 17 Moses led them out from the camp to meet with God, and they stood at the foot of the mountain. 18 All of Mount Sinai was covered with smoke because the Lord had descended on it in the form of fire. The smoke billowed into the sky like smoke from a brick kiln, and the whole mountain shook violently. 19 As the blast of the ram's horn grew louder and louder, Moses spoke, and God thundered his reply. 20 The Lord came down on the top of Mount Sinai and called Moses to the top of the mountain. So Moses climbed the mountain.

Exodus 20:18–21

18 When the people heard the thunder and the loud blast of the ram's horn, and when they saw the flashes of lightning and the smoke billowing from the mountain, they stood at a distance, trembling with fear.

19 And they said to Moses, "You speak to us, and we will listen. But don't let God speak directly to us, or we will die!"

20 "Don't be afraid," Moses answered them, "for God has come in this way to test you, and so that your fear of him will keep you from sinning!"

21 As the people stood in the distance, Moses approached the dark cloud where God was.

Moses and the people had an opposite
reaction to God's mighty presence.
The people retreated from God,
while Moses drew nearer to God.
Where do you find yourself in this story?

Terry Teykl, *The Presence Based Church*

"To see a person's face is to gaze into the window of their presence. When we seek God's Presence, we are seeking his face or his countenance. We are seeking to know him as we might know our spouse or our child. Being 'face to face' or touching a person's face is a very intimate, vulnerable experience."[9]

SCRIPTURE & READING REFLECTION:

Entry Date: _____

_____

_____

_____

_____

_____

_____

_____

_____

_____

_____

_____

_____

_____

_____

_____

EXERCISE & PRAYER TIME REFLECTION:

SURRENDERING

WEEK THREE

WEEK THREE EXERCISES

These exercises may be done in any order.
Check the box when completed!
An explanation of each exercise can
be found in the following pages.

☐ Soaking Prayer, 30+ minutes

☐ Immersion Prayer, Call to Samuel

☐ Night Watch Prayer. 30+ minutes

☐ Fasting from Speaking, 6+ hours

☐ Identify Idolatry, 20+ minutes

EXERCISE 1: Soaking Prayer, 30+ mins

You may find you are getting better at ignoring distractions by this point. You also may not need a song or Scripture to help you focus on the Lord. Record if and when this transition happens. As you rest in God's presence, what can you hear Him speaking into your spirit?

"He may come in a quiet whisper. Or He will paint a picture in your mind that would startle you or trigger thoughts and emotions that would release joy unspeakable. . . . Sometimes He overwhelms you with His love flowing like liquid fire into your being consuming fears, doubts, limitations, rejections, shame, and making you free. There will be times you feel deep peace, or His glory comes like a weighty substance that covers your entire body."[1]

Leif Hetland & Paul Yadao, *Soaking in God's Presence*

EXERCISE 2: Immersion Prayer, 15+ mins

Call to Samuel, 1 Samuel 3:1–18

This prayer time immerses your imagination in the Scripture. Picture yourself in the room with Samuel and Eli. How would it feel to hear your name repeatedly as Samuel does, then to realize it is the Lord calling you? How would you respond? How might your senses be heightened during this conversation?

EXERCISE 3: Night Watch Prayer, 30+ mins

Sometime between the hours of 2 a.m. and 5 a.m., set your alarm to get you out of bed for at least 30 minutes of prayer.

"Hearing God's voice today is a very natural act but requires the activity of a supernatural God. There is no autopilot setting that guarantees that you will hear. One truth is that if you do nothing, you will receive nothing. But the seemingly opposite truth is also true: When you least qualify and least expect it, God shows up!"[2]

James Goll, *Hearing God's Voice Today*

EXERCISE 4: Fasting from Speaking, 6+ hrs

Find a 6+ hour block to remain silent. You may still be doing work around the house, but refrain from playing music, having the television on, or being in public. If your family or spouse is home, perhaps you can do this together. This time of silence is meant to show us the needless ways we speak and how rarely we silence the chatter to truly listen to God.

"What needs to be guarded is the life of the Spirit within us. Especially we who want to witness to the presence of God's Spirit in the world need to tend to the fire within with utmost care. It is not so strange that many ministers have become burnt-out cases, people who say many words and share many experiences, but in whom the fire of God's Spirit has died and from whom not much more comes forth than their own boring, petty ideas and feelings. . . .

Our first and foremost task is faithfully to care for the inward fire so that when it is really needed it can offer warmth and light to lost travelers. . . .

. . . But silence is a sacred discipline, a guard of the Holy Spirit."[3]

Henri Nouwen, *The Way of the Heart*

EXERCISE 5: Identify Idolatry, 20+ mins

"Invite the Presence of God and ask Him to show you any area of your life that is separating you from Him. As He identifies areas of your life that need attention, write them down. When you are satisfied you have heard fully from God, go to Psalm 78 and make note of all the ways you can counter any tendencies to idolatry in your life. . . . Idolatry can and will creep back into our lives and must be constantly identified and dealt with in order to live from a place of God's Presence."[4]

Heidi and Rolland Baker, *Living from the Presence*

Conclude by reflecting on Philippians 3:7-9.
[7] I once thought these things were valuable, but now I consider them worthless because of what Christ has done. [8] Yes, everything else is worthless when compared with the infinite value of knowing Christ Jesus my Lord. For his sake I have discarded everything else, counting it all as garbage, so that I could gain Christ [9] and become one with him.

Bob Sorge, *Secrets of the Secret Place*

"If you will seek Him with all your heart, He will guide you to the ancient river that runs deep in the heart of God. As you chase Him with every ounce of your strength, He will bring you to the fountain of divine life. When the life of God begins to flow into your world of impossibilities, this is the stuff of miracles. The life of God cannot be stopped! If you drink of this river, everything in you and around you will begin to shake and shudder under the groundswell of God's power released."[5]

¹ Oh, the joys of those who do not
follow the advice of the wicked,
or stand around with sinners,
or join in with mockers.
² But they delight in the law of the Lord,
meditating on it day and night.
³ They are like trees planted along the riverbank,
bearing fruit each season.
Their leaves never wither,
and they prosper in all they do.

Trees planted along the riverbank bear spiritual
fruit in and out of season. When we pursue
God's presence, wisdom and direction,
we are able to navigate circumstances whether
in a season of chaos or rest.

How are you learning to connect to
the deep flowing river of God in
your every day life?

SCRIPTURE & READING REFLECTION:

Entry Date: _____

_____

_____

_____

_____

_____

_____

_____

_____

_____

_____

_____

_____

_____

_____

_____

EXERCISE & PRAYER TIME REFLECTION:

Leif Hetland, *Transformed by Love*

"Sometimes things don't go the way we expect them to. Businesses fail, ministries fall apart, relationships become damaged beyond repair, and people die. Disappointment can come from many different places, but the result is often the same, a lack of hope. . . .

Too often, as Christians, we feel the need to be perfect in the presence of our creator. . . .

Mistakenly, we attribute this same need for everything to be 'fine' to God. We feel that we are not permitted to tell God that we are disappointed or angry, especially if that anger or disappointment is directed at Him. . . .

We don't need to hide our disappointments. Hiding them under a smiling mask will only cause our wounds to fester. We need to be honest with ourselves, each other, and God. Then God will have an opportunity to remind us of who He is, and that will build our faith. . . .

Being vulnerable isn't always easy, even being vulnerable with God. However, vulnerability sets the table for love. . . .

. . . find a quiet place and speak to the Father about any pains or disappointments you have in your life. They could be fresh, or situations from a long time ago. He's not afraid to bring old things up if needed. Speak your true feelings to Him, but know that He loves you more than anyone or anything else could."[6]

[1] O Lord, I have come to you for protection; don't let me be disgraced.
Save me, for you do what is right.
[2] Turn your ear to listen to me; rescue me quickly. Be my rock of
protection, a fortress where I will be safe.
[3] You are my rock and my fortress. For the honor of your name, lead me
out of this danger.
[4] Pull me from the trap my enemies set for me, for I find protection in you
alone.
[5] I entrust my spirit into your hand. Rescue me, Lord, for you are a faithful
God.

Psalm 62:1–2

[1] I wait quietly before God, for my victory comes from him.
[2] He alone is my rock and my salvation, my fortress where I will never be
shaken.

SCRIPTURE & READING REFLECTION:

Entry Date: _____

_____

_____

_____

_____

_____

_____

_____

_____

_____

_____

_____

_____

_____

_____

_____

_____

EXERCISE & PRAYER TIME REFLECTION:

_____

_____

_____

_____

_____

_____

_____

_____

_____

_____

_____

_____

_____

_____

_____

In Tozer's *Knowledge of the Holy*, he explains ways in which we must prepare our hearts to gain more of God's presence. He lists: having a repentant heart, commitment to the life of faith, a complete surrender to be formed by Christ, turning away from idols, the practice of loving meditation upon God, and freely sharing this love and presence of God with others.[7]

A. W. Tozer, *Knowledge of the Holy*

"First, we must forsake our sins. . . .

Second, there must be an utter committal of the whole life to Christ in faith. . . .

Third, there must be a reckoning of ourselves to have died unto sin and to be alive unto God in Christ Jesus, followed by a throwing open of the entire personality to the inflow of the Holy Spirit. . . .

Fourth, we must boldly repudiate the cheap values of the fallen world and become completely detached in spirit from everything that unbelieving men set their hearts upon, allowing ourselves only the simplest enjoyments of nature which God has bestowed alike upon the just and unjust."[8]

¹⁷ This means that anyone who belongs to Christ has become a new [creation]. The old life is gone; a new life has begun!

¹⁸ And all of this is a gift from God, who brought us back to himself through Christ. And God has given us this task of reconciling people to him. ¹⁹ For God was in Christ, reconciling the world to himself, no longer counting people's sins against them. And he gave us this wonderful message of reconciliation. ²⁰ So we are Christ's ambassadors; God is making his appeal through us. We speak for Christ when we plead, "Come back to God!" ²¹ For God made Christ, who never sinned, to be the offering for our sin, so that we could be made right with God through Christ.

What do you need to surrender
to live into your rightful inheritance
as a new creation?

SCRIPTURE & READING REFLECTION:

Entry Date: _____

_____

_____

_____

_____

_____

_____

_____

_____

_____

_____

_____

_____

_____

_____

EXERCISE & PRAYER TIME REFLECTION:

DAY 14

4 "Listen, O Israel! The Lord is our God, the Lord alone. 5 And you must love the Lord your God with all your heart, all your soul, and all your strength. 6 And you must commit yourselves wholeheartedly to these commands that I am giving you today. 7 Repeat them again and again to your children. Talk about them when you are at home and when you are on the road, when you are going to bed and when you are getting up. 8 Tie them to your hands and wear them on your forehead as reminders. 9 Write them on the doorposts of your house and on your gates."

John Wesley, "*Spiritual Worship (1780)*"

In Wesley's sermon "Spiritual Worship" written around the age of 77, he says, "You cannot find your long sought happiness in all the pleasures of the world . . . You cannot find it in the religion of the world, either in opinions or a mere round of outward duties. Vain labour! Is not 'God a spirit'? . . . In this alone can you find the happiness you seek—in the union of your spirit with the Father of spirits; in the knowledge and love of him who is the fountain of happiness, sufficient for all the souls he has made."[9]

How might you become more wholehearted
in your love of the Lord
and in seeking after Him?

SCRIPTURE & READING REFLECTION:

Entry Date: _____

_____

_____

_____

_____

_____

_____

_____

_____

_____

_____

_____

_____

_____

_____

_____

_____

EXERCISE & PRAYER TIME REFLECTION:

C. S. Lewis, *The Weight of Glory*

"The promise of glory is the promise, almost incredible and only possible by the work of Christ, that some of us, that any of us who really chooses, shall actually survive that examination, shall find approval, shall please God. To please God . . . to be a real ingredient in the divine happiness . . . to be loved by God, not merely pitied, but delighted in as an artist delights in his work or a father in a son—it seems impossible, a weight or burden of glory which our thoughts can hardly sustain. But so it is."[10]

[1] O God, you are my God; I earnestly search for you. My soul thirsts for
    you; my whole body longs for you in this parched and weary land
    where there is no water.

[2] I have seen you in your sanctuary and gazed upon your power and glory.

[3] Your unfailing love is better than life itself; how I praise you!

[4] I will praise you as long as I live, lifting up my hands to you in prayer.

[5] You satisfy me more than the richest feast. I will praise you with songs of
    joy.

[6] I lie awake thinking of you, on you through the night.

[7] Because you are my helper, I sing for joy in the shadow of your wings.

[8] I cling to you; your strong right hand holds me securely.

How does it feel to know God delights in you?
How might you respond?

SCRIPTURE & READING REFLECTION:

Entry Date: _____

_____

_____

_____

_____

_____

_____

_____

_____

_____

_____

_____

_____

_____

_____

_____

_____

EXERCISE & PRAYER TIME REFLECTION:

LISTENING

WEEK FOUR

WEEK FOUR EXERCISES

These exercises may be done in any order.
Check the box when completed!
An explanation of each exercise can
be found in the following pages.

☐ Soaking Prayer, 30+ minutes

☐ Immersion Prayer, Shepherd's Voice

☐ Night Watch Prayer, 30+ minutes

☐ Fasting from Food, 24 hours

☐ Gratitude Worship, 20+ minutes

EXERCISE 1: Soaking Prayer, 30+ mins

Are any distractions persisting? Are you finding this 30+ minutes is not dragging as it once was? As you rest in God's presence, what can you hear Him speaking to your spirit?

"God's Presence comes in waves. Be sensitive to the flow of the Holy Spirit within you. Watch out for impressions rising within your heart as the Spirit of God leads you deeper. What I like about soaking is this: it is never boring. . . . As our hearts and our thoughts focus on Him, our whole being responds to Him—our emotions, desires, creativity, passion, faith and dreams are awakened."[1]

Leif Hetland & Paul Yadao, *Soaking in God's Presence*

EXERCISE 2: Immersion Prayer, 15+ mins

Shepherd's Voice, John 10:1–18

This prayer time immerses your imagination in the Scripture. Picture yourself as a member of the crowd or a disciple hearing this teaching for the first time. Picture the actual relationship between a shepherd and his sheep. How might you better distinguish between the voice of Jesus, the lies of the enemy, the wisdom of the world, and your own inclinations?

EXERCISE 3: Night Watch Prayer, 30+ mins

Sometime between the hours of 2 a.m. and 5 a.m., set your alarm to get you out of bed for at least 30 minutes of prayer.

"If you want to hear His comforting voice, you have to listen to His convicting voice. And it's often what we want to hear *least* that we need to hear *most*. Trust me, though, you want to hear what He has to say. Are you ready? Here's the seven-word prayer that can change your life: 'Speak, Lord, for your servant is listening.' That is easier said than done, no doubt. But if you meant what you just prayed, your life is about to change for the better."[2]

Mark Batterson, *Whisper*

EXERCISE 4: Fasting from Food, 24 hrs

You may do this a number of ways, depending on your health and physical ability. You may decide to fast from solid food, and still drink limited amounts of juice and water. You may fast from all food except a meal at dinner. If you have certain health issues, please consult a doctor before fasting from food. The timeline is also flexible. You may decide to fast from sun down to sun down (i.e. 6 p.m. to 6 p.m.).

The goal of this fast is to go without something in order to refocus our attention on the Lord. When we feel a hunger pain, it reminds us of Jesus and all he sacrificed for us. As Goll mentions below, fasting for him is a time of getting in touch with God's heart and mind.

> Ask God to make you more sensitive to His voice, promptings and presence.

"When properly understood and practiced, fasting is both a powerful weapon of spiritual warfare and an indispensible aid for entering into intimacy with God. It is also a key to releasing God's presence in and through our lives. Because it helps us get in touch with God's heart and mind, fasting also assists us in preparing ourselves for the outward ministry of sharing the fire of God's love with others."[3]

James Goll, *The Lost Art of Practicing His Presence*

EXERCISE 5: Gratitude Worship, 15+ mins

Make a list of all that you are grateful for, one side for items of this world, and the other for aspects of God. In other words, one column would focus on your family, health, etc. and the other column would list God's goodness, love, etc. Then give God thanks for all that you have written.

"Gratitude is a loving and thankful response toward God for his presence with us and within the world. Though 'blessings' can move us into gratitude, it is not at the root of a thankful heart. Delight in God and his good will is the heartbeat of thankfulness."[4]

Adele Ahlberg Calhoun, *Spiritual Disciplines Handbook*

Mark Batterson, *Whisper*

"God often speaks loudest when we are quietest."[5]

"Prayer is the difference between the best we can do and the best God can do. But there is something even more important and powerful than *talking* to God. What is it? *Listening* to God. It turns a monologue into a dialogue, which is exactly what He wants.

 I have a simple rule of thumb when I meet with someone: do more listening than talking. The more I want to hear what the person has to say, the quieter I am. What's a good rule of thumb with God.

 Lean into His whisper. Then pray the bravest prayer!"[6]

⁹ But the Lord said to him, "What are you doing here, Elijah?"

¹⁰ Elijah replied, "I have zealously served the Lord God Almighty. But the people of Israel have broken their covenant with you, torn down your altars, and killed every one of your prophets. I am the only one left, and now they are trying to kill me, too."

¹¹ "Go out and stand before me on the mountain," the Lord told him. And as Elijah stood there, the Lord passed by, and a mighty windstorm hit the mountain. It was such a terrible blast that the rocks were torn loose, but the Lord was not in the wind. After the wind there was an earthquake, but the Lord was not in the earthquake. ¹² And after the earthquake there was a fire, but the Lord was not in the fire. And after the fire there was the sound of a gentle whisper. ¹³ When Elijah heard it, he wrapped his face in his cloak and went out and stood at the entrance of the cave.

What chaos or distractions need to be turned off in your life to hear God's whisper?

SCRIPTURE & READING REFLECTION:

Entry Date: _____

EXERCISE & PRAYER TIME REFLECTION:

A. W. Tozer, *Knowledge of the Holy*

"Knowledge of such a Being cannot be gained by study alone. It comes by wisdom the natural man knows nothing of, neither can know, because it is spiritually discerned. To know God is at once the easiest and the most difficult thing in the world. It is easy because it is freely given. As sunlight falls free on the open field, so to the knowledge of the holy God is a free gift to men who are open to receive it. But this knowledge is difficult because there are conditions to be met and the obstinate nature of fallen man does not take kindly to them."[7]

What sort of conditions do you think Tozer is referencing?

¹ Honor the Lord, you heavenly beings; honor the Lord for his glory
and strength.

² Honor the Lord for the glory of his name. Worship the Lord in the
splendor of his holiness.

³ The voice of the Lord echoes above the sea. The God of glory
thunders. The Lord thunders over the mighty sea.

⁴ The voice of the Lord is powerful; the voice of the Lord is majestic.

⁵ The voice of the Lord splits the mighty cedars; the Lord shatters the
cedars of Lebanon.

⁶ He makes Lebanon's mountains skip like a calf; he makes Mount
Hermon leap like a young wild ox.

⁷ The voice of the Lord strikes with bolts of lightning.

⁸ The voice of the Lord makes the barren wilderness
quake; the Lord shakes the wilderness of Kadesh.

⁹ The voice of the Lord twists mighty oaks and strips the forests bare.
In his Temple everyone shouts, "Glory!"

¹⁰ The Lord rules over the floodwaters. The Lord reigns as king forever.

¹¹ The Lord gives his people strength. The Lord blesses them with peace.

This Scripture highlights the power of
the voice of the Lord.
How would you describe God's voice?

SCRIPTURE & READING REFLECTION:

Entry Date: _____

_____

_____

_____

_____

_____

_____

_____

_____

_____

_____

_____

_____

_____

_____

EXERCISE & PRAYER TIME REFLECTION:

DAY 18

J. Oswald Sanders, *Enjoying Intimacy with God*

"In the sacred discourse in the upper room, when Jesus bared His heart to His disciples, He stressed the necessity and possibility of maintaining the closest, most intimate fellowship with himself. . . .

Abiding in Christ is, of course, possible only to real Christians. It means keeping unbroken contact with Christ in a union of intimate love. The word abide means simply 'to remain, to stay, to continue, to cling to.' It is as though the Lord was saying, 'When you believed in me, you were united to me. Don't allow anything to break that intimate union. Keep constantly depending on me. . . .'

. . . 'Apart from Me,' said Jesus, 'you can do nothing' (v. 5). The absoluteness and finality of the statement is staggering. Not 'very little,' but 'nothing.' Cut off from the source of life-giving sap, we wither and die. . . ."[8]

> But then Jesus calls us friends,
> and we are no longer servants.

"Friends are friends because they share common tastes, ideals, and objectives. They share secrets with perfect confidence. Slaves do not share secrets with their masters, but friends do so with their friends. Their relationship is relaxed and without inhibition. They find each other's company congenial. What a breathtaking conception of our relationship with our Lord!"[9]

¹ "I am the true grapevine, and my Father is the gardener. ² He cuts off every branch of mine that doesn't produce fruit, and he prunes the branches that do bear fruit so they will produce even more. ³ You have already been pruned and purified by the message I have given you. ⁴ Remain in me, and I will remain in you. For a branch cannot produce fruit if it is severed from the vine, and you cannot be fruitful unless you remain in me.

¹² "This is my commandment: Love each other in the same way I have loved you. ¹³ There is no greater love than to lay down one's life for one's friends. ¹⁴ You are my friends if you do what I command. ¹⁵ I no longer call you slaves, because a master doesn't confide in his slaves. Now you are my friends, since I have told you everything the Father told me. ¹⁶ You didn't choose me. I chose you. I appointed you to go and produce lasting fruit, so that the Father will give you whatever you ask for, using my name. ¹⁷ This is my command: Love each other."

How can your relationship with Jesus more closely resemble a friendship?

What would be required to maintain that type of relationship?

SCRIPTURE & READING REFLECTION:

Entry Date: _____

_____

_____

_____

_____

_____

_____

_____

_____

_____

_____

_____

_____

_____

_____

_____

_____

_____

_____

EXERCISE & PRAYER TIME REFLECTION:

Bill Johnson, *Face to Face with God*

In a section titled "All Can Perceive," Bill Johnson writes, "Through Christ, God has made it possible for every person to see the kingdom. Our conversion gives us access to that realm, as Jesus explained to Nicodemus, 'Most assuredly, I say to you, unless one is born again, he cannot see the kingdom of God' (John 3:3, NKJV). However, it is our responsibility to develop this capacity, to train our senses to perceive God through renewing our minds and feeding the affections of our hearts on the truth. Otherwise, we will have no internal paradigm to keep us in tune with the truth amid the prevailing cultural attitudes that surround us."[10]

God reveals His kingdom to help us understand what is true. Without this revelation, how might we be confused?

Proverbs 3:5–6

5 Trust in the Lord with all your heart;
   do not depend on your own understanding.
6 Seek his will in all you do,
   and he will show you which path to take.

Joel 2:28–29

28 "Then, after doing all those things,
I will pour out my Spirit upon all people.
Your sons and daughters will prophesy.
Your old men will dream dreams,
and your young men will see visions.
29 In those days I will pour out my Spirit
even on servants—men and women alike."

SCRIPTURE & READING REFLECTION:

Entry Date: _____

_____

_____

_____

_____

_____

_____

_____

_____

_____

_____

_____

_____

_____

_____

_____

_____

EXERCISE & PRAYER TIME REFLECTION:

Exodus 34:29

29 When Moses came down Mount Sinai
carrying the two stone tablets inscribed
with the terms of the covenant,
he wasn't aware that his face had become
radiant because he had spoken to the Lord.

When we spend time with the Lord, we start to
transform and radiate God's presence.
How have you felt this happening
during these recent weeks?

Isaiah 55:8-9

8 "My thoughts are nothing like your thoughts," says the Lord.
"And my ways are far beyond anything you could imagine.
9 For just as the heavens are higher than the earth,
so my ways are higher than your ways
and my thoughts higher than your thoughts."

The Lord's wisdom is so much greater than our
own. How are you seeking His wisdom for
situations in your life?

James Goll, *Hearing God's Voice Today*

"The New Testament teaches us that we can have the 'mind of Christ' (1 Corinthians 2:16). But there is a noticeable gap between our thoughts, opinions, reasoning and traditions, and His. We are unaccustomed to His ways. We think He should do things in a certain order, and He seems to like to mess that up. God's guidance might not seem to be very pleasant, because we experience heartbreak and disappointment.

Sometimes the voice of the Lord and His guidance system is like that proverbial sand in the oyster. It is an irritant to begin with. But give it some time and room to do its work, and a pearl of great price will emerge.

If we choose His way over our way, it might seem painful for the moment, but the end result will be good."[11]

What pearls is God working on in your life?

SCRIPTURE & READING REFLECTION:

Entry Date: _____

_____

_____

_____

_____

_____

_____

_____

_____

_____

_____

_____

_____

_____

_____

_____

_____

_____

_____

EXERCISE & PRAYER TIME REFLECTION:

EXPLORING

WEEK FIVE

WEEK FIVE EXERCISES

These exercises may be done in any order.
Check the box when completed!
An explanation of each exercise can
be found in the following pages.

☐ Soaking Prayer, 30+ minutes

☐ Immersion Prayer, Calming the Storm

☐ Night Watch Prayer, 30+ minutes

☐ Fasting from Speaking, 6+ hours

☐ Outside Praise, 20+ minutes

EXERCISE 1: Soaking Prayer, 30+ mins

"Focusing on the Lord also means to have an expectant heart for Him to come, much like a watchman waiting for the breaking of dawn. We focus our whole being with a deep sense of anticipation and excitement. We pay close attention in our spirit for whatever God has for us. The moment God shows up, we are ready to plunge into His Presence and not let go of Him. . . .

. . . There will be times when you will sense that your emotions, desires, joys and peace are being awakened as you allow Him to guide you deeper into the Presence of God."[1]

Leif Hetland & Paul Yadao, *Soaking in God's Presence*

EXERCISE 2: Immersion Prayer, 15+ mins

Calming the Storm, Matthew 8:23–27

This prayer time immerses your imagination in the Scripture. Picture yourself in the boat with the disciples and Jesus. What would the environment be like to make them this terrified? How would this make you feel? What is it like to see Jesus perform this miracle? Are you filled with awe, fear, amazement? How is Jesus desiring to calm a storm in your life?

EXERCISE 3: Night Watch Prayer, 30+ mins

Sometime between the hours of 2 a.m. and 5 a.m., set your alarm to get you out of bed for at least 30 minutes of prayer.

"Basically, to center down means to recognize the center of quiet in the midst of the storm in our soul—kind of like the eye of the hurricane . . .

For most of us this center of quiet is not easy to find. Although quietness before God 'cannot be hurried or forced,' and 'must be allowed to happen,' it will not come automatically. We must consciously desire it, deliberately plan for it, and diligently pursue it. The rewards of success will justify all the time, energy, effort, and rigorous self-discipline required to get there. We will be at peace in the presence of the Lord."[2]

James Goll, *The Lost Art of Practicing His Presence*

EXERCISE 4: Fasting from Speaking, 6+ hrs

Find a 6+ hour block to remain silent. You may still be doing work around the house, but refrain from playing music, having the television on, or being in public. If your family or spouse is home, perhaps you can do this together. This time of silence is meant to show us the needless ways we speak and how rarely we silence the chatter to truly listen to God.

"But let us not be too literal about silence. After all, silence of the heart is much more important than silence of the mouth. Abba Poemen said: 'A man may seem to be silent, but if his heart is condemning others he is babbling ceaselessly. But there may be another who talks from morning till night and yet he is truly silent.'

Silence is primarily a quality of the heart that leads to ever-growing charity. Once a visitor said to a hermit, 'Sorry for making you break your rule.' But the monk answered, 'My rule is to practice the virtue of hospitality towards those who come to see me and send them home in peace.'

Charity, not silence, is the purpose of the spiritual life and of ministry."[3]

Henri Nouwen, *The Way of the Heart*

EXERCISE 5: Outside Praise, 20+ mins

Take some time to either walk or sit outside and praise your Heavenly Father. As you walk or sit, look around you. What does God highlight? What wonders are there to behold? What illustrations is He showing you? This is a time of both prayer and praise. Ask God to help you have awe in His presence, power, and goodness. This is a perfect time to engage all of your senses as you pray. What do you smell, see, feel, and hear? Also, feel free to speak out loud to God as you pray and praise.

If possible, try to find a place that is not overpowered with man-made noise.

Brother Lawrence, *Practicing the Presence of God*

Brother Lawrence referring to himself in the third person, as to not appear prideful and yet share his experience, says, "I know a person who for forty years has practiced the presence of God, to which he gives several other names. Sometimes he calls it a simple act—a clear and distinct knowledge of God—and sometimes he calls it a vague view or a generation, loving look at God—a remembrance of Him. He also refers to it as attention to God, silent communion with God, confidence in God, or the life and the peace of the soul. . . .

My friend says that by dwelling in the presence of God he has established such a sweet communion with the Lord that His spirit abides, without much effort, in the restful peace of God. In this center of rest, he is filled with a faith that equips him to handle anything that comes into his life.

This is what he calls the 'actual presence' of God, which includes any and all kinds of communion a person who still dwells on earth can possibly have with God in heaven. At times, he can live as if no one else existed on earth but himself and God. He lovingly speaks with God wherever he goes, asking Him for all he needs and rejoicing with Him in a thousand ways.

Nevertheless, one should realize that this conversation with God occurs in the depth and center of the soul. It is there that the soul speaks to God heart to heart and always dwells in a great and profound peace that the soul enjoys in God."[4]

How have you experienced conversation
with God in the center of your soul?

How is this peace related to the firm
foundation in this Scripture below?

Luke 6:47–49

47 "I will show you what it's like when someone comes to me, listens to my teaching, and then follows it. 48 It is like a person building a house who digs deep and lays the foundation on solid rock. When the floodwaters rise and break against that house, it stands firm because it is well built. 49 But anyone who hears and doesn't obey is like a person who builds a house right on the ground, without a foundation. When the floods sweep down against that house, it will collapse into a heap of ruins."

SCRIPTURE & READING REFLECTION:

Entry Date: _____

_____

_____

_____

_____

_____

_____

_____

_____

_____

_____

_____

_____

_____

_____

_____

_____

_____

_____

EXERCISE & PRAYER TIME REFLECTION:

James Goll, *Hearing God's Voice Today*

"Have you ever seen or felt or discerned a supernatural presence by the Holy Spirit—whether it be angelic or a demonic one? When we 'see' or 'sense' or 'feel' a spiritual entity nearby, we have *discerned* its presence. Hebrews 5:14 (NASB) says, 'But solid food is for the mature, who because of practice have their senses trained to discern good and evil.' This is about the training of our senses, which help us discern. They are a key component to the process.

Surrendering our senses to the Holy Spirit involves the very act of presenting the members of our physical body to God (see Romans 6:13, 19). We sanctify each of our five natural senses to the Holy Spirit. We surrender everything we have to Him to be used for His divine purposes."[5]

God can communicate to us using any of our senses, whether smelling a fragrance, seeing a vision, hearing a whisper, sensing a touch, or tasting the Lord's Supper.

How have you experienced God through your senses?

[1] I will praise the Lord at all times. I will constantly speak his praises.

[2] I will boast only in the Lord; let all who are helpless take heart.

[3] Come, let us tell of the Lord's greatness; let us exalt his name together.

[4] I prayed to the Lord, and he answered me. He freed me from all my fears.

[5] Those who look to him for help will be radiant with joy; no shadow of
    shame will darken their faces.

[6] In my desperation I prayed, and the Lord listened; he saved me from all
    my troubles.

[7] For the angel of the Lord is a guard; he surrounds and defends all who
    fear him.

[8] Taste and see that the Lord is good. Oh, the joys of those who take
    refuge in him!

[9] Fear the Lord, you his godly people, for those who fear him will have all
    they need.

[10] Even strong young lions sometimes go hungry, but those who trust in
    the Lord will lack no good thing.

[11] Come, my children, and listen to me, and I will teach you to fear
    the Lord.

[12] Does anyone want to live a life that is long and prosperous?

[13] Then keep your tongue from speaking evil and your lips from telling lies!

[14] Turn away from evil and do good. Search for peace, and work to
    maintain it.

SCRIPTURE & READING REFLECTION:

Entry Date: _____

_____

_____

_____

_____

_____

_____

_____

_____

_____

_____

_____

_____

_____

_____

_____

_____

EXERCISE & PRAYER TIME REFLECTION:

Francis Chan, *Crazy Love*

"When you are truly in love, you go to great lengths to be with the one you love. You'll drive for hours to be together, even if it's only for a short while. You don't mind staying up late to talk. Walking in the rain is romantic, not annoying. You'll willingly spend a small fortune on the one you're crazy about. When you are apart from each other, it's painful, even miserable. He or she is all you think about; you jump at any chance to be together."[6]

How can our pursuit of God more closely resemble Chan's illustration above?

Song of Solomon 8:6–7

6 Place me like a seal over your heart,
like a seal on your arm.
For love is as strong as death,
its jealousy as enduring as the grave.
Love flashes like fire,
the brightest kind of flame.
7 Many waters cannot quench love,
nor can rivers drown it.
If a man tried to buy love
with all his wealth,
his offer would be utterly scorned.

SCRIPTURE & READING REFLECTION:

Entry Date: _____

_____

_____

_____

_____

_____

_____

_____

_____

_____

_____

_____

_____

_____

_____

_____

EXERCISE & PRAYER TIME REFLECTION:

_____

_____

_____

_____

_____

_____

_____

_____

_____

_____

_____

_____

_____

_____

DAY 24

Heidi and Rolland Baker, *Reckless Devotion*

"We need to position ourselves so we keep on being filled, so we are in the right place to continue receiving the blessings of God. . . .

Holy Spirit will keep pouring Himself out as long as people are willing to be filled and willing to be poured out themselves—as long as He can find those who are wholly given over to God to be used for His purposes.

God will keep pouring out His presence as long as there are vessels to be filled. But He can't pour out where there is nothing to contain His presence."[7]

How have you prepared your heart
to be poured into by God?

5 You see, we don't go around preaching about ourselves. We preach that Jesus Christ is Lord, and we ourselves are your servants for Jesus' sake. 6 For God, who said, "Let there be light in the darkness," has made this light shine in our hearts so we could know the glory of God that is seen in the face of Jesus Christ.

7 We now have this light shining in our hearts, but we ourselves are like fragile clay jars containing this great treasure. This makes it clear that our great power is from God, not from ourselves.

8 We are pressed on every side by troubles, but we are not crushed. We are perplexed, but not driven to despair. 9 We are hunted down, but never abandoned by God. We get knocked down, but we are not destroyed. 10 Through suffering, our bodies continue to share in the death of Jesus so that the life of Jesus may also be seen in our bodies.

How does being filled with God
help us during times of trial?

SCRIPTURE & READING REFLECTION:

Entry Date: _____

_____

_____

_____

_____

_____

_____

_____

_____

_____

_____

_____

_____

_____

_____

_____

_____

EXERCISE & PRAYER TIME REFLECTION:

DAY 25

Genesis 28:11-17

11 At sundown [Jacob] arrived at a good place to set up camp and stopped there for the night. Jacob found a stone to rest his head against and lay down to sleep. 12 As he slept, he dreamed of a stairway that reached from the earth up to heaven. And he saw the angels of God going up and down the stairway.

13 At the top of the stairway stood the Lord, and he said, "I am the Lord, the God of your grandfather Abraham, and the God of your father, Isaac. The ground you are lying on belongs to you. I am giving it to you and your descendants. 14 Your descendants will be as numerous as the dust of the earth! They will spread out in all directions—to the west and the east, to the north and the south. And all the families of the earth will be blessed through you and your descendants. 15 What's more, I am with you, and I will protect you wherever you go. One day I will bring you back to this land. I will not leave you until I have finished giving you everything I have promised you."

16 Then Jacob awoke from his sleep and said, "Surely the Lord is in this place, and I wasn't even aware of it!" 17 But he was also afraid and said, "What an awesome place this is! It is none other than the house of God, the very gateway to heaven!"

Bill Johnson, *Face to Face with God*

"Jacob's conclusion to his first encounter with God is remarkable. . . .

It's possible to be right next to God and not know it! I often see this truth played out in my own life. It never ceases to amaze me that in the same meeting one person can be experiencing a powerful touch from the Lord, and at the same moment the person next to him is wondering when the meeting will be over so he can go to lunch.

There are two things that we should learn from this fact. The first thing to realize is that it is possible to position ourselves to encounter God by learning to recognize the signs of His presence, not only as we experience them but also as others experience them. . . .

The second thing to realize is that when God does lift the veil of our senses to perceive what is going on in the spiritual realm, we are not spectators who have stumbled upon something that has nothing to do with us. God is communicating with us and allowing us to see what He sees in order to invite us to know Him and partner with what is He is doing.

It is a mistake to think that only certain people with unique gifts can hear and see God."[8]

Looking back, how have you missed
opportunities for God
to speak to you?

SCRIPTURE & READING REFLECTION:

Entry Date: _____

_____

_____

_____

_____

_____

_____

_____

_____

_____

_____

_____

_____

_____

_____

_____

EXERCISE & PRAYER TIME REFLECTION:

REFLECTING

WEEK SIX

WEEK SIX EXERCISES

These exercises may be done in any order.
Check the box when completed!
An explanation of each exercise can
be found in the following pages.

☐ Soaking Prayer, 30+ minutes

☐ Immersion Prayer, David Dancing

☐ Night Watch Prayer, 30+ minutes

☐ Fasting: From Food, 24 hours

☐ Praise Worship, 30+ minutes

EXERCISE 1: Soaking Prayer, 30+ mins

"As we soak with the right heart, His words become seeds sown in our hearts. As we choose to remain in His presence, the seeds will surely yield a great harvest – thirty, sixty and hundredfold."[1]

"The goal of soaking prayer is communion and intimacy. It is a coming to God face to face. The focus is God and not self. We come for God Himself, and not to ask for the answers to our needs. . . . Developing intimacy with God warrants time. It takes time to go deep. Communion is taking the time to search His heart and allowing our hearts to be yielded and open to His inner workings. As we alight our hearts to His, we hear His voice and experience Him deeper."[2]

Leif Hetland & Paul Yadao, *Soaking in God's Presence*

Reflect on how your experience of soaking prayer has changed over these last weeks.

EXERCISE 2: Immersion Prayer, 15+ mins

David Dancing, 2 Samuel 6:12–22

This prayer time immerses your imagination in the Scripture. Picture yourself as David in this story. What amount of joy must you be feeling to dance as freely as David? How would it feel to have people observing this uninhibited praise and dancing? What does it feel like to dance this way before the Lord?

Included in the reading is Michal's remarks to David. How has fear of what people think inhibited your public and private worship?

EXERCISE 3: Night Watch Prayer, 30+ mins

Sometime between the hours of 2 a.m. and 5 a.m., set your alarm to get you out of bed for at least 30 minutes of prayer.

How have these midnight prayers surprised you?

"Oh, let me tell you how much God desires our presence. How much God longs to hear from us. How much God yearns to communicate with us. At the very heart of God is the passionate disposition to be in loving fellowship with you . . . with me."[3]

Richard Foster, *Sanctuary of the Soul*

"To awaken to faith, the Holy Spirit will take us through times when the presence of God cannot be clearly discerned. The Lord's goal during these times is to bring to maturity our spiritual senses.

Therefore do not accept that God has permanently hidden self from you, though during trials it may seem so. He is teaching us to see in the dark and to hear in the silence. He is making Himself known to our inner man so that, regardless of outer circumstances, we can continually be led by His Spirit.

. . . Never mistake temporary darkness for permanent blindness, for today's training is the very process that opens us to see God's glory."[4]

Francis Frangipane, *I Will Be Found by You*

How do Frangipane's words encourage you?

EXERCISE 4: Fasting from Food, 24 hrs

As noted before, the goal of this fast is to go without something in order to refocus our attention on the Lord.

How have these times of fasting been fruitful?

EXERCISE 5: Praise Worship, 30+ mins

This worship is a time to either sing, dance or both. In the privacy of your own home and when you will not feel the prying eye of others, let your inhibitions go and worship freely like King David. If you are not a singer, then move your body. If your mobility is limited, then you could raise your arms instead. Put on inspiring worship music and show your Father how much you love Him.

1 Corinthians 13:1-7

[1] If I could speak all the languages of earth and of angels, but didn't love others, I would only be a noisy gong or a clanging cymbal. [2] If I had the gift of prophecy, and if I understood all of God's secret plans and possessed all knowledge, and if I had such faith that I could move mountains, but didn't love others, I would be nothing. [3] If I gave everything I have to the poor and even sacrificed my body, I could boast about it; but if I didn't love others, I would have gained nothing.

[4] Love is patient and kind. Love is not jealous or boastful or proud [5] or rude. It does not demand its own way. It is not irritable, and it keeps no record of being wronged. [6] It does not rejoice about injustice but rejoices whenever the truth wins out. [7] Love never gives up, never loses faith, is always hopeful, and endures through every circumstance.

This is a well known Scripture, often read at weddings. However, in the Greek there are four different words for love, and this passage is not referring to the romantic kind of love.

This passage uses 'agape' love, which is a covenantal love between God and His people.

How does that change how you read this passage? This love is something God desires we return to Him, with the help of the Holy Spirit.

J. Oswald Sanders, *Enjoying Intimacy with God*

"Love is the fruit of the Spirit. That fruit is not the product of painful striving, but of simple abiding in Christ, as earlier noted. Indeed, each element in the fruit of the Spirit (Galatians 5:22-23) is but a different facet of love. Joy is love's song. Peace is love's repose. Patience is love's endurance. Kindness is love's sympathy. Goodness is love's self-forgetfulness. Faithfulness is love's trustworthiness. Self-control is love's discipline."[5]

SCRIPTURE & READING REFLECTION:

Entry Date: _____

_____

_____

_____

_____

_____

_____

_____

_____

_____

_____

_____

_____

_____

_____

_____

EXERCISE & PRAYER TIME REFLECTION:

_____

_____

_____

_____

_____

_____

_____

_____

_____

_____

_____

_____

_____

_____

_____

_____

_____

DAY 27

Below is Brother Lawrence's ninth letter, writing to a sister in Christ about how even he feels he's squandered opportunities to become more like Christ.

Brother Lawrence, *Practicing the Presence of God*

"We can begin all over again and repair the lost opportunity, returning with complete confidence to this kind Father, who is always ready to receive us lovingly. . . .

. . . To be with Him, we must cultivate the holy habit of thinking of Him often.

. . . We have to know someone before we can truly love him. In order to know God, we must think about Him often. Once we get to know Him, we will think about Him even more often, because where our treasure is, there also is our heart!"[6]

Joseph de Beaufort, *Practicing the Presence of God*

Brother Lawrence's friend writes about him in the "Second Conversation," "He believed that God is much greater than any of the simple gifts He gives us. Rather than desiring them for Him, he chose to look beyond the gifts, hoping to learn more about God Himself."[7]

As Paul addresses the Gentiles of Athens, he explains the greatest pursuit and purpose for God's people.

ACTS 17:22–28

22 So Paul, standing before the council, addressed them as follows: "Men of Athens, I notice that you are very religious in every way, 23 for as I was walking along I saw your many shrines. And one of your altars had this inscription on it: 'To an Unknown God.' This God, whom you worship without knowing, is the one I'm telling you about.

24 "He is the God who made the world and everything in it. Since he is Lord of heaven and earth, he doesn't live in man-made temples, 25 and human hands can't serve his needs—for he has no needs. He himself gives life and breath to everything, and he satisfies every need.26 From one man he created all the nations throughout the whole earth. He decided beforehand when they should rise and fall, and he determined their boundaries.

27 "His purpose was for the nations to seek after God and perhaps feel their way toward him and find him—though he is not far from any one of us. 28 For in him we live and move and exist. As some of your own poets have said, 'We are his offspring.'"

SCRIPTURE & READING REFLECTION:

Entry Date: _____

_____

_____

_____

_____

_____

_____

_____

_____

_____

_____

_____

_____

_____

_____

EXERCISE & PRAYER TIME REFLECTION:

DAY 28

17 With the Lord's authority I say this: Live no longer as the Gentiles do, for they are hopelessly confused. 18 Their minds are full of darkness; they wander far from the life God gives because they have closed their minds and hardened their hearts against him. 19 They have no sense of shame. They live for lustful pleasure and eagerly practice every kind of impurity.

20 But that isn't what you learned about Christ. 21 Since you have heard about Jesus and have learned the truth that comes from him, 22 throw off your old sinful nature and your former way of life, which is corrupted by lust and deception. 23 Instead, let the Spirit renew your thoughts and attitudes. 24 Put on your new nature, created to be like God —truly righteous and holy.

As a child of the light, what is God revealing to you about your next steps after this devotion challenge?

John Stickl, *Follow the Cloud*

"If pressed to say what step God is asking you to take right now toward freedom, what would you say? It may be a huge, risky step, or it might be something incredibly simple."[8]

"At the heart of every next step God asks us to take is a revelation of more of Jesus."[9]

SCRIPTURE & READING REFLECTION:

Entry Date: _____

_____

_____

_____

_____

_____

_____

_____

_____

_____

_____

_____

_____

_____

_____

_____

_____

_____

_____

EXERCISE & PRAYER TIME REFLECTION:

Henri Nouwen, *The Way of the Heart*

"To pray always—this is the real purpose of the desert life. Solitude and silence can never be separated from the call to unceasing prayer. If solitude were primarily an escape from a busy job, and silence primarily an escape from a noisy milieu, they could easily become very self-centered forms of asceticism. But solitude and silence are for prayer. The Desert Fathers did not think of solitude as being alone, but as being alone with God. They did not think of silence as not speaking, but as listening to God."[10]

"In thinking about God, as with speaking to God, our frustration tolerance is quite low, and it does not take much to stop praying altogether. Reading a book or writing an article or sermon is a lot more satisfying than this mental wandering into the unknown. . . .

. . . The crisis of our prayer life is that our mind may be filled with ideas of God while our heart remains far from him. Real prayer comes from the heart."[11]

"This purity of heart allows us to see more clearly, not only our own needy, distorted, and anxious self but also the caring face of our compassionate God."[12]

How has God helped you to persevere
during these thirty days?

[4] One day Jesus told a story in the form of a parable to a large crowd that had gathered from many towns to hear him: [5] "A farmer went out to plant his seed. As he scattered it across his field, some seed fell on a footpath, where it was stepped on, and the birds ate it. [6] Other seed fell among rocks. It began to grow, but the plant soon wilted and died for lack of moisture. [7] Other seed fell among thorns that grew up with it and choked out the tender plants. [8] Still other seed fell on fertile soil. This seed grew and produced a crop that was a hundred times as much as had been planted!" When he had said this, he called out, "Anyone with ears to hear should listen and understand."

[9] His disciples asked him what this parable meant. [10] He replied, "You are permitted to understand the secrets of the Kingdom of God. But I use parables to teach the others so that the Scriptures might be fulfilled:

'When they look, they won't really see.
When they hear, they won't understand.'

[11] "This is the meaning of the parable: The seed is God's word. [12] The seeds that fell on the footpath represent those who hear the message, only to have the devil come and take it away from their hearts and prevent them from believing and being saved. [13] The seeds on the rocky soil represent those who hear the message and receive it with joy. But since they don't have deep roots, they believe for a while, then they fall away when they face temptation. [14] The seeds that fell among the thorns represent those who hear the message, but all too quickly the message is crowded out by the cares and riches and pleasures of this life. And so they never grow into maturity. [15] And the seeds that fell on the good soil represent honest, good-hearted people who hear God's word, cling to it, and patiently produce a huge harvest."

If your heart is the soil, how have you seen a change over the last six weeks? Year?

SCRIPTURE & READING REFLECTION:

Entry Date: _____

_____

_____

_____

_____

_____

_____

_____

_____

_____

_____

_____

_____

_____

_____

_____

_____

EXERCISE & PRAYER TIME REFLECTION:

DAY 30

Francis Frangipane, *I Will Be Found by You*

In Frangipane's section, "Highest Goal in Seeking God," he says, "Those who understand the ways of God know that many of the greatest realities God has for us are gifts He has hidden in His heart. To obtain these blessings, God must be sought. You see, the Lord not only desires to bless us, but He also wants us to draw near to Him. He wants us to discover and know His deep love for us.

Thus, the highest form of seeking God is not for personal needs or even for other people. There comes a time when we seek God for Himself. Maturity comes as we break the cycle of seeking God only during times of hardship. A touch from God is wonderful, but we are in pursuit of more than just an experience—more than 'goose bumps and tears.' We are seeking a place of abiding in Christ, where we are keenly aware of His presence within us."[13]

How does Frangipane's claim about the highest form of seeking God challenge your typical prayer time?

Read Proverbs 2, which speaks of the amazing wisdom and treasure to be found in seeking the Lord.

Proverbs 2:1–11

¹ My child, listen to what I say,
and treasure my commands.
² Tune your ears to wisdom,
and concentrate on understanding.
³ Cry out for insight,
and ask for understanding.
⁴ Search for them as you would for silver;
seek them like hidden treasures.
⁵ Then you will understand what it means to fear the Lord,
and you will gain knowledge of God.
⁶ For the Lord grants wisdom!
From his mouth come knowledge and understanding.
⁷ He grants a treasure of common sense to the honest.
He is a shield to those who walk with integrity.
⁸ He guards the paths of the just
and protects those who are faithful to him.
⁹ Then you will understand what is right, just, and fair,
and you will find the right way to go.
¹⁰ For wisdom will enter your heart,
and knowledge will fill you with joy.
¹¹ Wise choices will watch over you.
Understanding will keep you safe.

SCRIPTURE & READING REFLECTION:

Entry Date: _____

_____

_____

_____

_____

_____

_____

_____

_____

_____

_____

_____

_____

_____

_____

_____

EXERCISE & PRAYER TIME REFLECTION:

PROMPTINGS JOURNAL

dreams

visions

scriptures

convictions

& more

Record here any promptings you receive, whether in the form of Scripture, dreams, visions, convictions, clear words, physical sensations, songs in your head, and even those of which you are unsure.

It may be helpful to date these entries.

Entry Date:

Entry Date:

Entry Date:

Entry Date:

Entry Date:

Entry Date: _____

Entry Date:

Entry Date: _____

Entry Date: _____

Entry Date: _____

Entry Date:

Entry Date:

Entry Date: _____

Entry Date: _____

Entry Date:

Entry Date:

Entry Date:

Entry Date:

Entry Date: _____

Entry Date:

NOTES

WEEK 1: STARTING

1. Paul Yadao and Leif Hetland, *Soaking in God's Presence* (San Bernardino, CA: Global Mission Awareness, 2017), 23. globalmissionawareness.com

2. James W. Goll, *Hearing God's Voice Today: Practical Help for Listening to Him and Recognizing His Voice* (Bloomington, MN: Chosen Books, 2016), 134–135. www.godencounters.com

3. Henri J. M. Nouwen, *The Way of the Heart* (New York, NY: Ballantine Books, 2003), 48–49.

4. John Wesley, "Upon Our Lord's Sermon on the Mount, VI (1748)," *John Wesley's Sermons: An Anthology*, ed. Albert Cook Outler and Richard P Heitzenrater (Nashville, TN: Abingdon Press, 1991), 226.

5. John Wesley, *A Plain Account of Christian Perfection* (Orlando, FL: Relevant Books, 2006), 5.

6. Michael Lombardo, *Immersed in His Glory: A Supernatural Guide to Experiencing and Abiding in God's Presence* (Shippensburg, PA: Destiny Image Publishers, Inc., 2018), 67. www.lifepouredoutintl.org

7. Michael Lombardo, *Immersed in His Glory*, 212.

8. A. W. Tozer, *God's Pursuit of Man: Tozer's Profound Prequel to The Pursuit of God*, Abridged ed. (Chicago, IL: Moody Publishers, 2015), 40–41.

9. John Stickl, *Follow the Cloud: Hearing God's Voice One Next Step at a Time* (Colorado Springs, CO: Multnomah, 2017), 49–50.

10. Terry Teykl and Lynn Ponder, *The Presence Based Church* (Muncie, IN: Prayer Point Press, 2003), 120. www.prayforrenewal.org

11. Tozer, *God's Pursuit of Man*, 25.

WEEK 2: RETREATING

1. Yadao and Hetland, *Soaking in God's Presence*, 27–28.

2. Goll, *Hearing God's Voice Today*, 137.

3. Goll, *Hearing God's Voice Today*, 84.

4. Michal Ann Goll, *A Call to the Secret Place* (Shippensburg, PA: Destiny Image Publishers, Inc., 2011), 20–21.

5. Teykl, *The Presence Based Church*, 78.

6. Lombardo, *Immersed in His Glory*, 33.

7. Lombardo, *Immersed in His Glory*, 36.

8. Richard Foster. *Prayer: Finding the Heart's True Home* (London, UK: Hodder & Stoughton, 2008), 107–108. renovare.org

9. Teykl, *The Presence Based Church*, 81.

WEEK 3: SURRENDERING

1. Yadao and Hetland, *Soaking in God's Presence*, 27.

2. Goll, *Hearing God's Voice Today*, 128.

3. Nouwen, *The Way of the Heart*, 47–48.

4. Heidi and Rolland Baker, *Living from the Presence: Interactive Manual* (Shippensburg, PA: Destiny Image Publishers, Inc., 2017), 126. rollandheidibaker.org

5. Bob Sorge, *Secrets of the Secret Place: Keys to Igniting Your Personal Time with God* (Lee's Summit, MO: Oasis House, 2001), 212. bobsorge.com

6. Leif Hetland, *Transformed by Love* (Peachtree City, GA: Global Mission Awareness, 2015), 107–111. globalmissionawareness.com

7. A. W. Tozer, *The Knowledge of the Holy* (San Francisco, CA: HarperOne, 1992), 115–116.

8. Tozer, *The Knowledge of the Holy*, 115–116.

9. John Wesley, "Spiritual Worship (1780)," *John Wesley's Sermons: An Anthology*, ed. Albert Cook Outler and Richard P. Heitzenrater (Nashville, TN: Abingdon Press, 1991), 440.

10. C. S. Lewis, *The Weight of Glory* (New York, NY: Touchstone Books, 1996), 54.

WEEK 4: LISTENING

1. Yadao and Hetland, *Soaking in God's Presence*, 27.

2. Mark Batterson, *Whisper: How to Hear the Voice of God* (Colorado Springs, CO: Multnomah, 2017), 2–3. www.markbatterson.com

3. James W. Goll, *The Lost Art of Practicing His Presence* (Shippensburg, PA: Destiny Image Publishers, Inc., 2005), 184. www.godencounters.com

4. Adele Ahlberg Calhoun, *Spiritual Disciplines Handbook: Practices That Transform Us*, revised and expanded ed. (Downers Grove, IL: InterVarsity Press, 2015), 31.

5. Batterson, *Whisper*, 14.

6. Batterson, *Whisper*, 20.

7. Tozer, *The Knowledge of the Holy*, 115.

8. J. Oswald Sanders, *Enjoying Intimacy with God* (Grand Rapids: MI: Discovery House Publishers, 2000), 61–63.

9. Sanders, *Enjoying Intimacy with God*, 66.

10. Bill Johnson, *Face to Face with God: The Ultimate Quest to Experience His Presence* (Lake Mary, FL: Charisma House, 2007), 89–90. bjm.org

11. Goll, *Hearing God's Voice Today*, 123.

WEEK 5: EXPLORING

1. Yadao and Hetland, *Soaking in God's Presence*, 25–26.

2. Goll, *The Lost Art of Practicing His Presence*, 24–25.

3. Nouwen, *The Way of the Heart*, 57.

4. Brother Lawrence, *The Practice of the Presence of God* (Springdale, PA: Whitaker House, 1982), 66–67.

5. Goll, *Hearing God's Voice Today*, 111.

6. Francis Chan and Danae Yankoski, *Crazy Love: Overwhelmed by a Relentless God* (Colorado Springs, CO: David C. Cook, 2008), 100. crazylove.org

7. Heidi and Rolland Baker, *Reckless Devotion: 365 Days into the Heart of Radical Love* (Minneapolis, MN: Baker Publishing Group, 2014), 163. rollandheidibaker.org

8. Johnson, *Face to Face with God*, 92–93.

WEEK 6: REFLECTING

1. Yadao and Hetland, *Soaking in God's Presence*, 30.

2. Yadao and Hetland, *Soaking in God's Presence*, 17–18.

3. Richard Foster, *Sanctuary of the Soul: A Journey into Meditative Prayer* (London, UK: Hodder & Stoughton, 2012), 15. renovare.org

4. Francis Frangipane, *I Will Be Found by You: Reconnecting with the Living God— the Key that Unlocks Everything Important* (Lake Mary, FL: Charisma House, 2013), 31–32.

5. Sanders, *Enjoying Intimacy with God*, 92.

6. Lawrence, *The Practice of the Presence of God*, 49.

7. Joseph de Beaufort, "Second Conversation," *The Practice of the Presence of God*, (Springdale, PA: Whitaker House, 1982), 13.

8. Stickl, *Follow the Cloud*, 27.

9. Stickl, *Follow the Cloud*, 22.

10. Nouwen, *The Way of the Heart*, 64.

11. Nouwen, *The Way of the Heart*, 69–71.

12. Nouwen, *The Way of the Heart*, 90.

13. Frangipane, *I Will Be Found by You*, 2–3.

ABOUT THE AUTHOR

In May of 2019, Rev. Madeline Carrasco Henners hopes to graduate from United Theological Seminary with a Doctor of Ministry. This devotional challenge served as one component of her thesis, and hopefully it will continue to prove helpful for those seeking to go deeper in intimacy with God and ability to hear God's voice.

Madeline's passion is helping people discover the amazing love God has for them. As her own spirit awakened to the deeper relationship God desired with her, she seeks to help others in their journey into God's heart. She is also passionate about the supernatural gifts of the Holy Spirit, offered to all God's children. She desires to continue growing in her ability to hear God's voice, especially as it helps others come to Christ.

Madeline is a United Methodist Elder, and she has served as a pastor in the Rio Texas Annual Conference area for over ten years. She graduated from Duke Divinity School with her Master of Divinity after completing her Bachelor of Arts from Southwestern University in Georgetown, TX. As a native Texan, Madeline grew up mostly in the Rio Grande Valley.

In 2007, she married her husband, David, who was born and raised in Liverpool, England. An architect by trade, David is an amazing ministry and prayer partner. Together, they seek to serve the Lord with all that they are.

Made in the USA
Lexington, KY
31 January 2018